T0368432

PRAYER MANUAL

Ben Foote

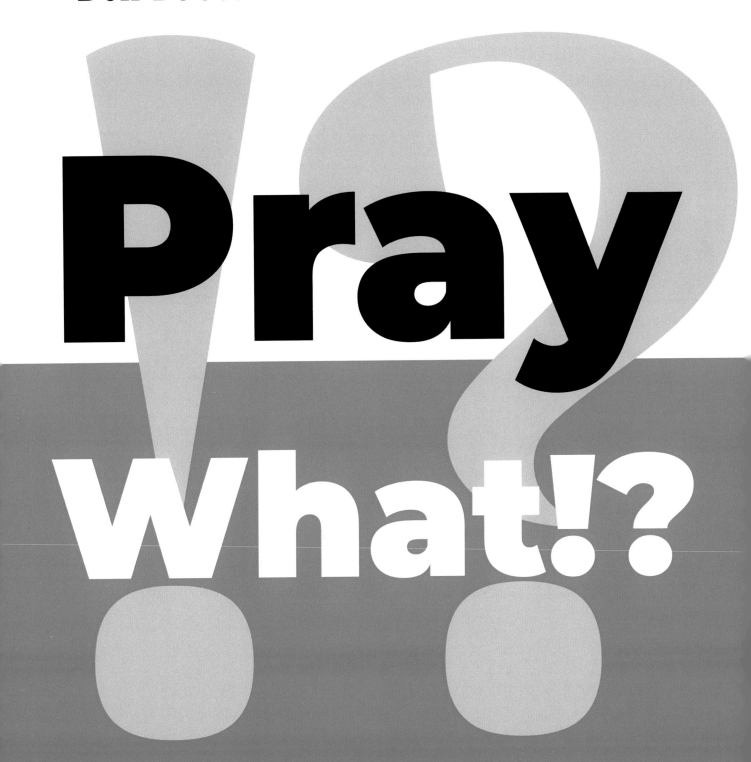

Pray

What!?

WORD VOICE REPENT FORGIVE WARFARE HEAL PROPHECY SPIRIT LEAD

In memory of my dear freind, Jeff Anderson, whose example of stepping out in bold faith when others see impossbility and hardship continues to inspire me to go wherever God leads. And my uncle Jon Foote, whose encouragemnt, laughter and ferocious passion for bringing the salvation of Jesus to others, drives God's purpose in my life to go beyond my own imagination.

Acknowledgments & Thanks

Amazing Journey and Amazing People

I had no idea the impact writing this book would have on me, and the connections God would make through others as I was writing, studying and testing this book. I want to thank each person that has encouraged, prayed and help develop this Prayer Manual into the resource it is today.

Specifically, for my amazing wife Laura, and your unending support to go where God leads us. For my mom, dad and grandparents, Barb, Al, Ron, June, Ted and Jane, along with my siblings and extended family; all of which follow Jesus and have set me up with a solid foundation to build on.

For my children and grandchildren, you are all a gift from God and the inspiration for me to continue in raising up the next generation for Christ.

For the first Pray What!? small group, Aprile, Clint, Connie, Dan, Deb, Deno, Jody, Kim, Lindsey, Mike and Ronda, having each one of you as part of this team is truly an honor and I will go to battle with you anytime.

For my Whitestone brothers, our walk together has helped bring me to the pinnacle of how God is using me. Thank you, Clif, Eric, Tony and Trevor.

For my mentors, Dave, Deb and Stephanie; Pastor Marty, Pastor Cub, Pastors Craig and Tommy; Cory, Keven, Ben, Kelly, and Ethan; all of you have been praying with me and for me in ways that have opened the doors of heaven so God is able to use me in ways I never even imagined.

Thank you, Pastor Louie Gigglio, for obediently delivering the call of God working miraculously in my life; Pastor Ketterling and Greg Youman of River Valley for proclaiming the call into prayer that God has placed on me; Pastor Samuel and Ron Graeff for the power of your prayer over me; Pastors Jacob & Hannah of Thrive Church and your prayer of blessing over me and my family; The Bridge Church, Jay Rudolph and the Algona Evangelical Free Church that have been instrumental in putting the gifts God has given me into practice.

To Lori and Laura for your editoral expertise and guidance.

And there are so many more that have been part of this journey. I thank you all and I know that this is only the beginning; there is so much more to come and we will pray together for the fulfillment of God's purpose in our lives as we look forward to our homecoming with Jesus.

Content

Preface: **what it's** all about

Pray What!? is to be a prayer manual, a guide to prayer introducing you into a dialogue with God, our Creator. It is intended to help teach you ways to have a deeper relationship with God through prayer. It will guide you and challenge you in ways that will open up new avenues of connection with Christ, through the power of the Holy Spirit. It will bring you and others together to pray for each other and with each other as we all strive to complete the mission that Jesus has given us.

As you go through this book, I would encourage you to dive into your own personal prayer life and go through it with others. As you journey through the chapters, the first four chapters build a solid foundation in order to equip you and activate the applications in the remaining chapters.

This prayer manual is intended to recruit and train teams of prayer warriors, prayer champions in the local church. It will bring us, as the Body of Christ, together in prayer as we pray for freedom, healing and encouragment for our communities, neighborhoods and homes. It will unify us as believers under the same banner of Christ as we march forward into the calling He has given each of us. It will train us as warriors for Christ, going to battle conquering the enemy that surrounds us, ready to destroy us every day.

Pray in the Spirit at all times and on every occasion. Stay alert and be persistent in your prayers for all believers everywhere - Ephesians 6:18 NLT

Pray God's Word

1

The importance of knowing God's Word, so many times is underrated by us. We tend to look first for the supernatural experience, the touchy feely goosebump experience. The things that cause chills to run up our spine, bring tears to our eyes and make us feel the presence of God right next to us, all around us. The feelings that inspire us to do better, be better, accomplish more than we thought we could, or maybe even wanted to. Those are all great, and I'm not downplaying them at all. God moves miraculously in those moments, and we see the jump start to life change in those amazing events. But what sets up those events to happen in the first place? What guides the leaders of amazing events to a great move of God? What solidifies the feelings of a powerful move of God to a consistent life change that lasts a lifetime?

God's Word is the key to unlocking blessing, provision and abundance of God in our lives. It is essential for us to sustain the fullness of God's presence in our lives. Knowing God's Word is what guides our prayer and forms our worship.

Praying in God's Word activates the promises He gives us in His Word. Having knowledge and wisdom of His Word keeps us focused on truth so we don't stray down the wrong path in pursuit of a feeling, but instead have a burning desire to be closer to God.

Matthew 5:18 NLT – I tell you the truth, until heaven and earth disappear, not even the smallest detail of God's law will disappear until its purpose is achieved.

God's Word is complete and absolute truth. His word guides us in what is right. His Word is reliable and in His Word is His presence. His Word speaks with us, in all circumstances.

His Word gives us life (Matthew 4:4 NLT)

His Word is perfect and pure (Psalms 12:6 NLT)

In our life and especially our prayer life, the Word of God is the bedrock for us to build on, the good soil for us to grow from. The solidity of His Word, the consistency of His promises, and the reliability of His faithfulness is the only thing that we can confidently anchor to. So, as things come against us and try to tear us down, we can stand on the firm foundation of the absolute truth of the Word of God. So, as we begin our journey into learning how to pray, we must first start with the Word of God.

Prayer isn't merely talking to or at God. It is talking WITH God. It is a conversation. As I've heard it described, "Prayer is meant to be a conversation between friends," and a conversation with a friend is so much more than talking to a friend - it involves including your friend in your thoughts, in what you are doing, and how you are feeling. Prayer needs to involve listening to God as well. It is God's voice that is by far the more important voice in our conversation. This means we need to know how to hear His voice. We should want to hear what He has to say, and understand how He feels about us, knowing that He knows what is best for us. Praying in the Spirit means we learn His voice and we listen to His voice.

God's Word is TRUE

● ● ●

2 Timothy 3:16-17 NLT

All Scripture is inspired by God and is useful to teach us what is true and to make us realize what is wrong in our lives. It corrects us when we are wrong and teaches us to do what is right. God uses it to prepare and equip His people to do every good work.

The first place that God speaks to us is in His Word, the Bible. The Bible is so much more than a collection of old books that have been collected. It is a collection of books inspired by the Holy Spirit to approximately 40 authors in a span of over 1,500 years. It is proven true by its own fulfillment of prophetic statements throughout the history of the earth, which are proven over and over again to be completely true. It is only when we understand the complete truth of the Bible that we can see our lives changed to align with the design of our Creator.

As we learn how to pray, how we are to converse with God, we see hundreds of examples of prayer in the Bible. There are over 650 prayers in the Bible, with 25 of those prayers by Jesus. So, when we are stuck in what to pray or how to pray, we can find examples of prayer in the Bible to model our prayer after.

The voice of God is always in alignment with Scripture. The Bible, the Word of God, is the ultimate test to anything that may be from God. If it aligns with God's Word, then it is of God. If it doesn't then it is of the enemy.

Knowing the voice of God and understanding His Word, how do we apply His Word in our life? The most powerful way to apply God's Word in your life is to pray it.

● **How do you pray? Write a brief description of how you pray.**

Prayers from the Bible:

Ephesians 1:15-18 NLT

Ever since I first heard of your strong faith in the Lord Jesus and your love for God's people everywhere, I have not stopped thanking God for you. I pray for you constantly, asking God, the glorious Father of our Lord Jesus Christ, to give you spiritual wisdom and insight so that you might grow in your knowledge of God. I pray that your hearts will be flooded with light so that you can understand the confident hope He has given to those He called—His holy people who are His rich and glorious inheritance.

John 17:20-24 NLT

I am praying not only for these disciples but also for all who will ever believe in Me through their message. I pray that they will all be one, just as You and I are one—as You are in Me, Father, and I am in You. And may they be in Us so that the world will believe You sent me.

I have given them the glory You gave Me, so they may be one as We are one. I am in them and You are in Me. May they experience such perfect unity that the world will know that You sent Me and that You love them as much as You love Me. Father, I want these whom You have given Me to be with Me where I am. Then they can see all the glory You gave Me because You loved Me even before the world began!

Pray Scripture

Read Psalm 100

● **Write Psalm 100 into a prayer:**

● **What is a significant Bible verse to you?**

● **Write that verse into a prayer.**

Pray
God's Voice

Prayer is an ongoing conversation with God and in any conversation, it involves listening as well as talking. To pray effectively we need to learn to hear His voice. We need to develop the discipline of listening to His voice. As we hear His voice and become familiar with it through prayer, then we grow our desire for prayer. This unlocks the part of prayer that grows a need for us to hear what He has to say, to know that He knows what is best for us and that who we are is found in who He says we are.

The ongoing theme of prayer is found in Ephesians 6:18 NLT, where we are to "Pray in the Spirit at all times and at every event." Praying in the Spirit includes learning to hear and listen to His voice. No matter our circumstance we can seek to listen in our struggle.

John 10:14 NLT – I am the good shepherd; I know My own sheep and they know Me.

Jeremiah 29:12 ESV – Call upon Me and come and pray to Me, and I will hear you.

One of the most important things we can do as we learn to hear His voice is to stop talking. To set our own things aside and simply listen. To open our hearts and allow Him to speak to us. The more we listen, the more we recognize His voice as He's speaking to us, whether we are in our own personal prayer time at home, praying and worshiping on our drive to work or praying with a friend. Including time to be quiet and listen is so powerful as it allows God to answer our prayers and even direct our prayers into the purpose He has for the situation we are praying for.

Prayer also includes knowing God is listening to us. He has promised us that when we pray to Him, He will listen to us. He hears us, sees us and knows our every need. He wants to hear our needs and desires from us. God wants us to have the confidence to come boldly to Him in prayer. Through Jesus Christ there does not need to be any separation between us and our Heavenly Father. So, we can confidently come into His presence knowing that He longs to hear our voice.

> **Hebrews 4:16 –** So let us come boldly to the throne of our gracious God. There we will receive His mercy, and we will find grace to help us when we need it most.
>
> **Psalm 5:3 -** In the morning, Lord, You hear my voice; in the morning I lay my requests before You and wait expectantly

As we seek to hear God's voice, it is helpful to understand how God hears our voice. Many times, we pray simply by speaking silently to God in our mind. Other times we may whisper our prayer, enough for us to hear the words we are making. Other times we pray out loud, whether with others or on our own, using the sound of our voice as we speak to God. There may be other times when we cry out to God, with a loud shout, with a weeping cry, or maybe in laughter of joy.

Talk With God

> **Philippians 4:6 NLT –** Don't worry about anything; instead, pray about everything. Tell God what you need, and thank Him for all He has done.

God wants us to bring all our needs to Him, without worry and with thankfulness. In the many ways we pray to Him, God also has many ways He speaks to us, when we are listening. He uses other people in our lives; He uses our own thought; sometimes He speaks in an audible voice; there are even accounts in the Bible where He's used animals to speak; and God uses Scripture. In fact, The Bible, God's Word always aligns with what He says through any other source. Regardless of what method He uses, we can test what we hear with His Word to assure that it is His voice we are hearing and not our own or the enemy's. The enemy would love to get our attention and make us believe that we are hearing God's voice when we are really listening to the enemy's or our own. Test what is said with the Bible to be sure that it is true.

Psalm 100 NLT - Shout with joy to the LORD, all the earth! Worship the LORD with gladness. Come before Him, singing with joy. Acknowledge that the LORD is God! He made us, and we are His. We are His people, the sheep of His pasture. Enter His gates with thanksgiving; go into His courts with praise. Give thanks to Him and praise His name. For the LORD is good. His unfailing love continues forever, and His faithfulness continues to each generation.

☐   **List the ways you talk with God:**

☐   **List things that help you focus on the conversation:**

God is Trustworthy

- In prayer ask God to speak to you and then listen for His voice. Describe God's voice and write what He is saying.

- Ask God for a Bible verse that will confirm or show you that it is God's voice that you hear. Write the verse below to align His Word with what He has spoken to you.

Pray
Repentance

As we develop our prayer life, praying for those that are lost is a place we go to often. We want to see our family, friends, neighbors, co-workers, doctors, etc. all come to know Jesus and have a personal relationship with Him. We pray that God would restore their lives to be close to Him. That God would restore broken marriages, heal broken hearts, restore communities, and bring a revival of the Holy Spirit into our city. We look to God to show up in people's lives in miraculous ways. Often, we may be praying for them every day.

What is it that brings that revival, that life change, that restoration that we pray for so fervently? The key to unlocking the door to restoration is repentance. It is the same key regardless of the restoration needed, whether it's in a relationship between husband and wife, or restoration of proper leadership in our city. Whether it's a restoration of a heart broken by addiction or the restoration of one that is lost and needs a relationship with their Heavenly Father. Repentance is the key to restoration to God.

> **2 Chronicles 7:14 NLT** – Then if My people who are called by My name will humble themselves and pray and seek My face and turn from their wicked ways, I will hear from heaven and will forgive their sins and restore their land.

The reason repentance is needed for restoration, is it removes what separates us from God. God wants and has provided for us the ability to live in complete communion with Him. We've been given the ability to live in the fullness of His blessing, all the time. What we have done is placed filters or veils between us and Him. In doing so we have blocked part and perhaps all the blessing of His presence. The thing we use as a veil is called sin. Sin prevents us from fully experiencing His blessing for us. Sin hinders us from realizing the greatness of who God is, and even more how His grace is available to remove the sin that is placed between us and Him.

In the Old Testament book of Exodus, (Exodus 19:16-20, 20:18, 26:33, 34:29-35) we see when the Israelites first came into the presence of God, God descended on the mountain before them, and His presence was so overwhelming they couldn't handle it. They begged Moses to meet with God for them, because they were afraid that His presence would kill them.

Sin - SEPARATES

●●●

Isaiah 59:2 ESV

But your iniquities have made a separation between you and your God, and your sins have hidden His face from you so that He does not hear.

Moses then went up to the mountain to be in God's presence, representing the people of Israel. When Moses came down from the mountain his face shown with the glory of God, so much so that the people were afraid of him and couldn't look at him. Moses had to wear a veil to separate them from the glory of God that shown on him, because of their fear.

The first structure built by the Israelites was used as a physical place of worship of the one true God, in which He instructs them to place a curtain or a veil between them and His presence. This was to protect them from the greatness of God's glory, His presence.

God instructed for a representative of His people to be cleansed and come into His presence once a year on behalf of His people. God's presence would rest in the Most Holy Place, separated from the people by a veil. Those full of sin remained separated from the full presence of God.

Matthew 27:50-51 ESV – And Jesus cried out again with a loud voice and yielded up His spirit. And behold, the curtain of the temple was torn in two, from top to bottom. And the earth shook, and the rocks were split.

Jesus, who is God in flesh, came to earth as a representative for us. He was without sin; He was always connected to God and God's glory. His sacrifice on the cross made a way for the veil of sin between us and God to be removed so we once again could walk freely, boldly without fear into the presence of God. By God's gift of grace through His son Jesus, His glory is available to us all the time. And the key to entering His presence is Repentance.

Hebrews 9:22 ESV – Indeed, under the law almost everything is purified with blood, and without the shedding of blood there is no forgiveness of sins.

Repent, which means turning around, turning from the way you were going and going the other way. With repentance we remove the veils we have placed between us and God who is always there, always available.

1 John 1:9 ESV – If we confess our sins, He is faithful and just to forgive us our sins and to cleanse us from all unrighteousness.

Perhaps you know someone that has never confessed and asked for forgiveness of their sins. For those of us that have acceepted God's gift of Grace through Jesus Christ, it is the most painful thing to experience when someone we love has not accepted that same gift. So, we pray that God, by the power of the Holy Spirit will call those that are lost to Himself and reveal His grace through Jesus Christ.

Or maybe you, yourself have never turned your life over to Christ by confessing your sins and asking Jesus to be the ruler of your life. And, that veil of sin is still in place, separating you from God. You can pray that prayer today, right now. Simply pray with your own words; "Lord God, I know I am a sinner and my sin separates me from my Creator. I want to be with you. I accept your gift of grace, by accepting the sacrifice of Your Son, Jesus Christ made on the cross in my place. Lord Jesus come into my life, wash away my sin, remove the veil and bring me into the family of God."

Turn Around

- **What are we to do or how do we receive the gift of grace given to us?**

With veils removed, God's presence becomes fully exposed in all His glory and we are restored back to Him. That's when broken lives are put back together. That's when a marriage that is torn to the point of divorce is mended and made whole. That's when communities that are divided by our own agendas are united in Christ. That's when someone who is on the brink of death from depression, addiction or abuse is brought back into the identity they have in Christ, restored as a child of God and resting in His Glory.

Name the Veils.

List the veils that you have placed between you and God. Next to the name of the veil write a Bible Verse that tears the veil apart.

VEIL: **VERSE:** _____
_____
_____

VEIL: **VERSE:** _____
_____
_____

VEIL: **VERSE:** _____
_____
_____

VEIL: **VERSE:** _____
_____
_____

VEIL: **VERSE:** _____
_____
_____

Write a prayer of repentance, naming each veil, removing the veil by proclaiming the blood of Jesus Christ and turning towards the presence of God.

Pray
Forgiveness

As prayer warriors we are often asked to pray for others. We pray that they would find freedom from various circumstances that they can't seem to break away from on their own. Many times we feel stuck, like no matter what we do we can't seem to get past a certain point and then we fail yet again. No matter how hard we try, we just can't seem to go any further.

We forget to use the key to freedom, which is forgiveness. Forgiveness is what breaks apart the chains that hold us down. Forgiveness breaks the ongoing repetitive failure that keeps happening over and over again. Forgiveness from God breaks the entrapment of Sin. This forgiveness is what Jesus, while on the cross, cried out to God in response to being tortured and crucified.

> **Luke 23:34a ESV – And Jesus said, "Father, forgive them, for they know not what they do."**

Jesus, while dying on the cross, had such a heart of forgiveness that He asked forgiveness for the ones that put Him there. Even without them asking for it or repenting of what they had done, Jesus still prayed for their forgiveness.

Many of us look at forgiveness as being the same as repentance, or that one is a prerequisite for the other. We talked previously about repentance and how repenting is turning away from where we were going and going the opposite direction. Our sin puts up veils between us and God. Repentance turns us to the fullness of His Glory.

Forgiveness is surrendering the wrong that is holding us down. Forgiveness removes the chains of unforgiveness that keep us stuck, unable to move past our own circumstance.

It is not someone else's forgiveness that frees us, but our forgiveness of others. As we forgive others, which can include ourselves, we release them to God and surrender our circumstance to Him. Through our surrender, God is able to do His great work in our lives, and the lives of those we forgive, bringing complete freedom to us.

> **Ephesians 4:25-27 ESV - Therefore, having put away falsehood, let each one of you speak the truth with his neighbor, for we are members one of another. Be angry and do not sin; do not let the sun go down on your anger and give no opportunity to the devil.**

Unforgiveness becomes a powerful weapon used by the enemy to keep us from moving beyond our own anger or resentment. If the enemy can keep our hearts from forgiving others, he effectively is able to keep us from being truly free. Unforgiveness breeds chains of anger, hatred, and pride that are hooked into our souls and the enemy. Satan uses those chains to manipulate us and intimidate us into the pit that keeps us from experiencing the freedom that Jesus has given us through His gift on the cross.

In the process of forgiveness there are six primary chains of unforgiveness that the enemy uses to keep control over our lives.

- Ask forgiveness of sin that has caused our circumstance
- Forgive those that have caused the hurt
- Forgive ourselves
- Forgive God and remove blame we placed on Him
- Forgiveness to our Inner-Child (Younger-Self), at the time our hurt occurred
- Forgiveness from our Inner-Child (Younger-Self), from the time our hurt occurred

As we ask and extend forgiveness in each area the chains of the enemy fall to the ground, unable to control us any longer.

With all chains of unforgiveness broken we are free to move forward and experience the freedom that God designed for us to have.

> **Repentance is Turning Around**
>
> **Forgiveness is Setting it Down**
>
> • • •
>
> **Mark 11:25 ESV And whenever you stand praying, forgive, if you have anything against anyone, so that your Father also who is in heaven may forgive you your trespasses.**

> **Ephesians 4:31-32 ESV - Let all bitterness and wrath and anger and clamor and slander be put away from you, along with all malice. Be kind to one another, tenderhearted, forgiving one another, as God in Christ forgave you.**

Is there a past hurt that you can't seem to get through? Write a brief summary of what has you stuck:

Identify all of those that were part of or affected by this hurt in your life. Be thorough and specific:

Pray through the six steps of forgiveness, releasing each one that you've identified with your own forgiveness. Remember, forgiveness is not agreeing with what happened, it is releasing the hurt from your grip and giving those that hurt you to God. As you pray, visualize each chain being unhooked from your spirit and dropping to the ground.

Process of Forgiveness

SIN		We ask forgiveness of any sin that we have done that has caused our circumstance.
HURT US		We forgive those that directly or indirectly hurt our or caused our circumstance.
OURSELVES		We forgive ourselves for the blame we have placed on ourselves, whether we are the cause or not.
GOD		We forgive God, not because God needs our forgiveness. We forgive God to remove any blame that we have placed on Him.
FOR INNER CHILD		We forgive ourselves at the time we were hurt; or another way to look at it, we as our current day self, forgive the younger us who is still stuck in that moment.
FROM INNER CHILD		We forgive ourselves from the time we were hurt; forgiving our inner child and removing any blame we placed on our inner child.

Pray Warfare

We are at War! We are constantly fighting for our families, our neighborhoods, our cities, our community, our lives. As we gain understanding of the battle we are in, we recognize that it is all around us, all the time. The enemy, Satan, is determined to destroy us, completely. No matter who we are or where we've come from. Satan doesn't care about our ethnicity, our age, our gender, our social status or economic position. He doesn't care what we believe. The enemy will use all resources available, including ourselves, to destroy all of humanity. That is his goal.

> **John 10:10a ESV** The thief only comes to steal, kill and destroy.

We stand on the side of victory, when we side with our Savior, Jesus Christ. Jesus loves us, completely. No matter who we are, no matter where we've come from, our ethnicity, our age, our gender, our social status or economic position, no matter what we believe, His love for us never stops. Jesus will use all resources available, including us, to call those that are lost into a relationship with Him. That is His purpose.

> **John 10:10b ESV** – I came that they may have life and have it abundantly.

This war that we are in, we tend to try and make it a fight against others, a fight with ideals, political opinions, even Bible theology and belief. We so easily turn the battle against each other, unaware that the battle isn't against each other but against Satan and his demons.

> **Ephesians 6:12 NLT - For we are not fighting against flesh-and-blood enemies, but against evil rulers and authorities of the unseen world, against mighty powers in this dark world, and against evil spirits in the heavenly places.**

We see the characteristic of the enemy in the weapons he uses. The very definition of who he is outlines the weapons of choice that he uses to destroy us. He is an angel filled with Pride (Ezekiel 28:17), he is a Sinner (1 John 3:8), he is an Accuser (Revelation 12:10), he is a Deceiver (2 Corinthians 11:3), he is a Murderer, he is the father of Lies (John 8:44), he is a Thief (John 10:10a), he is Defeated (Romans 16:20).

Armor of God

● ● ●

Truth
Righteousness
Peace
Faith
Salvation
Spirit/Word
Prayer

Satan's weapons of pride, temptation, deception, manipulation, and intimidation extend into each part of our lives, attempting to twist all that God has made good into a tool of destruction. These are not weapons that we can fight against in the physical world, but we must battle against them in the spiritual. The weapons we have been given to destroy Satan and his evil spirits are The Word of God, the Name of Jesus, and the Power of the Holy Spirit through our worship, praise and prayer.

> **Ephesians 6:13-18 NLT - Therefore, put on every piece of God's armor so you will be able to resist the enemy in the time of evil. Then after the battle you will still be standing firm. Stand your ground, putting on the belt of truth and the body armor of God's righteousness. For shoes, put on the peace that comes from the Good News so that you will be fully prepared. In addition to all of these, hold up the shield of faith to stop the fiery arrows of the devil. Put on salvation as your helmet, and take the sword of the Spirit, which is the word of God. Pray in the Spirit at all times and on every occasion. Stay alert and be persistent in your prayers for all believers everywhere.**

Of the seven pieces of armor, five of them are for our protection. And none of them protect our back. We are not to run from the fight, but run into it. Only two of them are offensive - the Sword, the Word of God that is sharper than any 2-edged sword (Hebrews 4:12), and Prayer. Prayer is what I consider the long-range weapon; I've heard it described as being the long-range ballistic missile of spiritual warfare. Prayer brings the full force of heaven against the enemy.

As we go to battle we will come against many of the evil spirits under Satan's command, known as demons. These demons are powerful, yes. But they are also powerless to the name of Jesus. Fighting these spirits with our own strength and without honoring the name of Jesus can lead to very bad results. We can read of an account of this in Acts 19:13-17.

We are not to fear any of these spirits - instead, we are to battle against them using the authority that we have been given in the name of Jesus Christ. With the power of the name of Jesus, demons tremble and flee. With the power of the name of Jesus we are used by Jesus to bring freedom to those that are being oppressed. The mention of the name of Jesus causes demons to bow to the one true King.

How do we use these weapons that are given to us?

How do we step onto the battlefield and claim the victory that is already ours?

We first recognize and identify the battle we are in. We might be fighting against fear, anger, depression, lust, pride, greed, or whatever is overtaking our lives and turning us away from God. We honestly see it and then we name it for what it is.

Once identified we can then recognize the lies that are being spoken into us; many times the enemy makes this sound like it's our own voice. We may be hearing lies like:
- "You aren't worth the effort - why do you even bother?"
- "No one understands you."
- "There's no way that you can do that."
- "You aren't good enough."
- "You don't need anyone - you can do this on your own."
- "You deserve more - you owe yourself."

And the list just keeps going, working to pull us down. But, when we list the lies and replace the lies with the truth of who you are in Christ, then we hear the truth:
- "You are a child of the King."
- "In God's strength all things are possible."
- "Your Creator love you - you are created for a purpose."
- "God's grace is enough."
- "God provides all you need."

We claim our victory by thanking God for all He's done, praising Jesus for who He is and inviting the Holy Spirit to fill us with His truth and love.

Philippians 2:9-11 NLT - Therefore, God elevated Him to the place of highest honor and gave Him the name above all other names, that at the name of Jesus every knee should bow, in heaven and on earth and under the earth, and every tongue declare that Jesus Christ is Lord, to the glory of God the Father.

Get in the Fight!

We aren't just made aware of the battle we are in, we are called to fight in it. Fight for our freedom. Fight for the Glory of God.

Write a battle that you are in right now:

_____

_____

Name the evil spirits that you are fighting against:

_____

_____

What lies has the enemy been speaking to you?

_____

_____

Proclaim the greatness of Jesus and command the spirits to leave in the name and authority of Jesus Christ. Then, ask the Holy Spirit to reveal His truth that cancels the lies of the enemy, and write those truths down:

_____

_____

Pray Healing

Healing prayer and the power of healing is such an amazing thing to witness. It is a gift given to us by the Holy Spirit. And as with all gifts from the Holy Spirit, He gives us these gifts as He sees fit. The gifts He gives are to grow our faith, encourage us and point others to Jesus. And to bring greater glory to God.

So many times in the Bible we see Jesus heal the sick, and often as He heals their physical illness, He also heals their soul in the process. He does the physical healing as a sign to others of who He is, in order to bring others to Him. He does the inner healing to bring the person being healed into a relationship with Him. Jesus heals in such a powerful way that they go and tell others of the greatness of who He is. In all healing, the primary purpose is to bring Glory to God and point to His love for us.

> **1 Corinthians 12:8-9 NLT -**
> **To one person the Spirit gives the ability to give wise advice (wisdom); to another the same Spirit gives a message of special knowledge. The same Spirit gives great faith to another, and to someone else the one Spirit gives the gift of healing.**

> **Matthew 16:25 - If you try to hang on to your life, you will lose it. But if you give up your life for My sake, you will save it.**

Inner healing is healing of wounds we carry because of the battles and attacks we have endured. Attacks of abuse, sin, curses, emotional stress, and soul ties to name a few.

To be healed of any of these inner wounds it takes a process of surrender, giving them all to Jesus. Jesus took care of all of these at the cross; we don't have to carry the burden of the wounds we have endured in our life. We can give them all to Jesus, who is waiting and will gladly take them.

This is able to be simple and immediate, but so many times we get ourselves in the way of the process. That's okay - that simply means that the process may take multiple times of surrendering our hurts and wounds to Christ.

It is the voicing of our wounds, to Christ and to others, that begins the healing process. If we are able to fully lay those at the feet of Jesus we can be completely healed from these inner wounds once and for all. It is when we decide to pick those hurts back up again that we find that we need to repeat the process of surrender to find complete healing.

Wounds & Hurts

•••

Abuse
Pride
Envy
Spoken Lies
Stress
Greed
Fear
Anger
Hate
Soul Ties
Sexual Sin

> **James 5:16 ESV - Therefore, confess your sins to one another and pray for one another, that you may be healed. The prayer of a righteous person has great power as it is working.**

This act of surrender includes the process of forgiveness. Going through the six steps of forgiveness, we break the chains that the enemy has attached to our wounds. In fact forgiveness is the part of the process that heals the scars from the wounds we have endured in our life. It is in the same method of the steps of forgiveness that we confess or acknowledge the hurts that we are experiencing in our soul. We name each wound and hand each of them over to Jesus. We then proclaim God's truth of who we are and allow Him to heal our wounds with the touch of His hand and the sound of His still small voice.

The other way we see Jesus bring healing is by healing our physical bodies, removing disease or illness, mending bones and muscle, loosening joints, reconnecting our mind, putting our body back into alignment with the way He designed. Through the power of the Holy Spirit He has made this gift of healing available to us.

It is important for us to understand why Jesus uses physical healing. What is the purpose for healing? One, he wants us to be healed. We read in the Bible many times that because of the compassion Jesus had on people He healed them. Also, the miracle of healing points non-believers to Christ, and it encourages and strengthens the faith of believers. And it always is to give glory to God. We shouldn't ever forget, it is because of Jesus' sacrifice on the cross that the power of healing is made available to us by the Holy Spirit.

We activate this gift of healing through the power of prayer. We pray for direct, specific healing by the power of the name of Jesus. These prayers shouldn't be complicated, but they should be with authority. It is the power of the Holy Spirit and the authority given to us by Jesus that brings the gift of healing to us. It is directed and distributed by the Holy Spirit, as He sees fit and for the glory of God.

As we pray for healing, we pray with boldness and expectancy, knowing that God desires to heal. He also knows all, and is above all things. His healing may not come in the way we want it to, or when we want it to. That doesn't mean He doesn't want us to ask for healing in the way we desire it to be. Healing prayer is not meant to be soft prayer or, as I describe them, "patty-cake" prayers. They are to be courageous, simple, faith filled, powerful prayers that are meant to unleash the healing power of the Holy Spirit. And as we pray, we receive the blessing of healing that is given, even if we aren't able to see the results in the moment.

Healing prayers also come with full surrender to the fact that His when, why and how are always better than our own. We acknowledge that God provides the healing by His method and timing; we can't take credit for it at all. The healing always points to Him, encouraging and growing our faith and drawing those that are lost to Him. And through it all we know Jesus is above it all.

Proclaim It!

1 Peter 3:22 NLT
Now Christ has gone to heaven. He is seated in the place of honor next to God, and all the angels and authorities and powers accept His authority.

Does someone you know need physical or inner healing? How can you pray for their healing? Write a prayer of healing for them:

Have you ever witnessed Jesus bring healing to someone, perhaps even yourself? If so, write a brief description of that experience:

How can you encourage them and use their healing to point them or others to Jesus?

Pray Prophecy

We all are given gifts as God sees fit, in His purpose and His timing, and for His glory. Each gift works in concert with the others. God's intent is that we work together as His Church and within His authority to bring freedom, encouragement, and blessing to our fellow believers. By activating the gifts given through prayer and exercising our gifts in obedience, we point others to Jesus in a life changing powerful way, a way that only a personal interaction with Christ can bring.

> **1 Corinthians 12:8-11 ESV - For to one is given through the Spirit the utterance of wisdom, and to another the utterance of knowledge according to the same Spirit, to another faith by the same Spirit, to another gifts of healing by the one Spirit, to another the working of miracles, to another prophecy, to another the ability to distinguish between spirits, to another various kinds of tongues, to another the interpretation of tongues. All these are empowered by one and the same Spirit, who apportions to each one individually as He wills.**

Prophecy throughout the Bible is God's voice revealing patterns or events, all with the intent of guiding us, encouraging us and showing us conclusive evidence of God's greatness. We tend to look at prophecy as foretelling the future. And yes, that is one aspect of prophecy. The Gift of Prophecy, that is given to us by the Holy Spirit, is given to us to encourage others in their walk with God. Prophecy is used to fill others up with the Joy, Hope & Love of God, through the power of the Holy Spirit. It is a gift given by the Holy Spirit, so we will speak the truth of the Holy Spirit to others, in order to lift each other up.

This gift of prophecy is like all other gifts given to us by the Holy Spirit. We activate it through prayer. We exercise through obedience and the declarations of prophecy do not contradict scripture. In fact many times I find that there is a direct scripture that is given with a prophetic word to further support and give greater insight to its meaning.

2 Peter 1:20-21 NLT - Above all, you must realize that no prophecy in Scripture ever came from the prophet's own understanding, or from human initiative. No, those prophets were moved by the Holy Spirit, and they spoke from God.

Has anyone ever given you an encouraging word?

•••

How did that help you?

1 Corinthians 13:8-10 NLT - Prophecy and speaking in unknown languages and special knowledge will become useless. But love will last forever! Now our knowledge is partial and incomplete, and even the gift of prophecy reveals only part of the whole picture! But when the time of perfection comes, these partial things will become useless.

It is important to remember that using the gift of prophecy only reveals part of the whole. That part that God gives us can be given in a variety of ways. Some are given pictures that describe or show a specific event, or image that symbolizes what God is pointing to. Others are given single words that have a specific meaning for the person they are meant for. Others are given phrases or even complete letters from God. And many times, certain verses are pointed to or revealed in the one giving or receiving the prophetic message. As this part of the whole picture is given, the purpose is that God is pointing us to see ourselves within the whole picture.

The whole picture is found in the Word of God that is revealed by the Holy Spirit and personified in Jesus Christ. All words of prophecy, given by the Holy Spirit, points us to Jesus, the complete Word of God. It is the Word of God that is eternal, that goes beyond the partial picture of prophecy.

Matthew 24:35 ESV
Heaven and earth will pass away, but My words will not pass away.

Psalm 118:105 ESV
Your word is a lamp to my feet and a light to my path.

We fine tune the gift of prophecy by being in the Word of God. It is knowing the Word of God that brings the gift of wisdom and knowledge, enabling the gift of prophecy to be exercised through us. It is by being in prayer that we are able to activate the gift of prophecy. It is by aligning our hearts with God, that He is able to effectively use us to strengthen and encourage others, giving the Church confidence in the power of the Holy Spirit as He works to unify us all in Christ. God uses this gift of prophecy to plant seeds into our hearts, seeds that produce an abundant harvest.

The gift of prophecy is like any other gift given to us by the Holy Spirit - it's given for us to use it. And like building a muscle of our body, it gets stronger with exercise. We first activate this gift with prayer. We exercise the gift of prophecy through obedience. God leads us in the prophetic words of encouragement for others. As we obediently deliever those words, His voice becomes clearer, and He entrusts us with greater prophecy for others. The important thing is to step out in faith and obey the prompting God is giving you. An encouraging message is only encouraging if it is delivered to the one the message is meant for. If we hold on to that message, it is unable to bless, guide and lift up the one that God is asking us to encourage.

Isaiah 55:11 NLT– **It is the same with My word. I send it out, and it always produces fruit. It will accomplish all I want it to, and it will prosper everywhere I send it.**

What words of prophecy have been spoken over you?

Have you seen them fulfilled?

God's Word
Produces fruit.

In prayer, ask God to reveal an encouraging word for someone in your life. Write down who He brings to mind and what He is showing you. It could be a picture, a movie scene, a single word, a series of words, a Bible verse, etc. Write it down and then take the time to deliver the message, in person if you can, although a phone call or text may be the best way to deliver it promptly. Exercise your gift through obedience.

If nothing is revealed to you, don't worry about it. It doesn't mean something is wrong with you. Keep asking, keep praying, keep listening. It may be that God is waiting for the right time, the right word for the right person to have its greatest impact on their life and yours.

Pray
Spirit

1 Corinthians 12 outlines how a spiritual gift is given to each of us so we can help each other. It is the one and only Spirit who distributes all these gifts. He alone decides which gift each person should have.

1 Corinthians 12:8-11 lists several of the gifts that the Holy Spirit gives us. We can find other lists of gifts in Isaiah 11:1-3, Romans 12:6-8 and Ephesians 4:11. All gifts are available and given to us to build up and encourage the body of Christ, His Church. We talked about the gift of prophecy and how the Holy Spirit gives that gift to encourage each other. Another gift given by the Holy Spirit is the gift of tongues, which is used in different ways. It's important to understand the different ways that the gift of tongues is used by the Holy Spirit. How it is sometimes used to strengthen others, and how that same gift is used other times to strengthen ourselves.

The gift of tongues is given so that we may have the ability to speak in a language that we have not learned but is understood as the language of others. This is what is described on the Day of Pentecost in Acts 2:4-12.

> **1 Corinthians 12:11 ESV** - All these [gifts] are empowered by one and the same Spirit, who apportions to each one individually as He wills.

Other times the gift of tongues is used where a person speaks in an unknown language for others to hear. When this is given by the Holy Spirit, it is always accompanied by the gift of interpretation. This is used to strengthen, direct and encourage people into what God is calling them to do.

The third way that the gift of tongues is given is as an unknown language between us and God. It is meant to be used in private, as a way for God to strengthen us as an individual.

1 Corinthians 14:2-4 NLT - For if you have the ability to speak in tongues, you will be talking only to God, since people won't be able to understand you. You will be speaking by the power of the Spirit, but it will all be mysterious. But one who prophesies strengthens others, encourages them, and comforts them. A person who speaks in tongues is strengthened personally, but one who speaks a word of prophecy strengthens the entire church.

This gift of tongues, when used as a personal resource of strength, is often called a "prayer language." A prayer language is used to not only find encouragement for us, but also to provide a Holy Spirit guided prayer when we don't know what to pray. The Holy Spirit intervenes for us and through the language that we cannot speak in words, and aligns our prayer with the heart of God.

The benefit of a prayer language is the Holy Spirit strengthening us, giving us the ability to connect with God in a different way. Using the gift of tongues in prayer puts our heart in a deeper level of surrender. It places our complete trust in the Holy Spirit as we pray, because we aren't relying on our own words but on the intercession of the Holy Spirit for us to our Heavenly Father.

To be clear, not having a prayer language does not mean that we aren't good at prayer, or that we are not connected to God. It is another gift and way to connect with God, but as Paul writes in 1 Corinthians 14:15-19 NLT, yes, we should desire to and "pray in the spirit" or in our prayer language, but there are other gifts that we should desire first, like the gift of prophecy, which is used to benefit other believers.

Romans 8:26-27 NLT - And the Holy Spirit helps us in our weakness. For example, we don't know what God wants us to pray for. But the Holy Spirit prays for us with groanings that cannot be expressed in words. And the Father who knows all hearts knows what the Spirit is saying, for the Spirit pleads for us believers in harmony with God's own will.

Have you been given a prayer language?

Would you like to have one?

Fruit of the Spirit

As we've talked about many of the gifts of the Holy Spirit and how we activate those gifts through prayer, we see how those gifts help strengthen and encourage each other. As we implement these gifts, focusing on God's Word and staying connected with God in prayer and worship, that is how we see the harvest of fruit in the lives around us.

When things in the spiritual are focused on confusion, chaos, anger, bitterness, resentment and pride, the fruit (or weeds) of those things are seen in our world as hate, jealousy, mistrust, depression, greed, loss of identity, loss of freedom, and loss of life.

> **Galatians 5:19-21 NLT -** When you follow the desires of your sinful nature, the results are very clear: sexual immorality, impurity, lustful pleasures, idolatry, sorcery, hostility, quarreling, jealousy, outbursts of anger, selfish ambition, dissension, division, envy, drunkenness, wild parties, and other sins like these. Let me tell you again, as I have before, that anyone living that sort of life will not inherit the Kingdom of God.

When what we are doing in the spiritual is focused on God's Word, praise, thanksgiving and worship of our Creator - when we have a humble heart and surrender to His design, praying in the spirit at all times - then we see a harvest of love, joy, peace, patience, kindness, goodness, faithfulness, gentleness, and self-control in our friends, families and neighbors. We see the hope that is found in Christ take over our communities and the abundant blessing of living our lives according to the design of the Designer.

> **Galatians 5:22 NLT -** But the Holy Spirit produces this kind of fruit in our lives: love, joy, peace, patience, kindness, goodness, faithfulness, gentleness, and self-control. There is no law against these things!

It all comes down to the condition of our heart - do we have a heart of surrender where we allow God to work in and through our lives? If so, we will see a harvest of the fruits of the Spirit in our lives. Then we are able to be used by the Holy Spirit to point others to Christ. Then we are filled, strengthened and renewed by the Holy Spirit, able to be poured out for others.

We are created in God's image (Genesis 1:27 ESV), meaning we are the only being created with three parts - body, soul and spirit. The body is our physical being, the soul is our mind and emotions, and our spirit is our connection with God. We tend to live our lives as though we have a spirit and soul living in a physical body. God's designed us as a spiritual being, with a soul and body that we use to accomplish the spiritual purpose He created us for. Through prayer, connecting with God, being in His Word and striving to exercise what God has given us through obedient use of His gifts we step into the spiritual world we are created to be connected to. We are able to be used by God to bring others into His wonderful plan of reconnection with our Creator, filled with the abundant fruit of the Holy Spirit.

Romans 12:2 NLT
Don't copy the behavior and customs of this world, but let God transform you into a new person by changing the way you think. Then you will learn to know God's will for you, which is good and pleasing and perfect.

Time to Garden!

What weeds do you need to remove so more fruit can grow?

_____

_____

_____

What fruit have you produced and what effect is that having on others?

_____

_____

_____

Pray Leading

We've been given the gifts, the tools necessary to partner with God in His purpose for us and for others. We know that, building on the foundation of His Word, we stand firm against the storms that come our way. We can stand firm for others as they weather through the storms of their lives. We have the gifts of the Holy Spirit, pouring out the encouragement, the joy, hope and love that only comes from Him. We are fully armed and ready to fight to protect others from the schemes of the devil, trying to destroy us. We have been given the keys to restoration and freedom and can walk with others as they search to find healing and freedom in their lives.

We are called to lead others in prayer, point others to the truth of God's Word, and reveal the love of Jesus to each one that we encounter. God has gifted us with many gifts to help those in need, those that are broken and lost.

> ## Romans 12:13 NLT
>
> **When God's people are in need, be ready to help them. Always be eager to practice hospitality.**

To answer the call to lead others in prayer, we first must have a soft heart that is prepared to hold others in the light of grace and truth. In the same way that we prepare our house for guests to arrive, we prepare our hearts to be fully open before God. With repentance we remove any veils that would get between us and God, so we can hear His voice and see His face. We keep our hearts always prepared, ready for battle by praying together, lifting each other up and lifting ourselves up as we pray in the Spirit.

> **Job 11:13-15 ESV** - If you prepare your heart, you will stretch out your hands toward Him. If iniquity is in your hand, put it far away, and let not injustice dwell in your tents. Surely then you will lift up your face without blemish; you will be secure and will not fear.

As leaders in prayer, we are called to step into a gap for others as we intercede in prayer. In bridging that gap it is essential that we have a heart of surrender. We are to rely on the victory that we can only find in Jesus. It is not by our own power, or our own understanding that we are able to stand in the gap. It is only through Jesus that we are able to stand, and it is to Him that we are to bring our heart of surrender.

> **Proverbs 3:5-6 NLT** – Trust in the LORD with all your heart; do not depend on your own understanding. Seek His will in all you do, and He will show you which path to take.

As prayer ministers, we are stepping onto the battlefield, fighting for others. We are to remain battle ready at all times. It is imperative that we stay alert, keeping each other covered in prayer. We keep our swords sharpened as we stay consistently in God's Word. We are called to encourage each other, guide each other and hold each other to the standard that Christ exemplified for us.

> **Ephesians 6:18 NLT** - Pray in the Spirit at all times and on every occasion. Stay alert and be persistent in your prayers for all believers everywhere.

As we go to battle, remember it isn't people we are at war with, it is the evil spirits of this dark world. This is a spiritual battle, not a physical one. We go into battle by activating the gifts of the Holy Spirit through prayer. We exercise those gifts by our obedience and grow confidence in the gifts given to us through studying the truth of God's Word. As we battle against the enemy, we find our strength in our love for Jesus and our love for each other.

It is the fullness of the Love of Christ that shines His light on us, pushing away the darkness of the world and bringing the Kingdom of Heaven into our presence. It is His light that we are to put on a lampstand for all to see. His light shines within with the presence of the Holy Spirit. It is His light that guides us as we pray with others.

When we pray for others, there are some key things we can do so others feel at ease and are open to receive all that God has to offer them as we partner with them in prayer. First, we simply state their name, showing the personal connection that God has with each of us through prayer. As we state their name, we are able to identify who they are in Christ. Simply by proclaiming their identity of who they are in Christ is a powerful and uplifting act of kindness, that opens up doors so the Holy Spirit can do His work.

We listen to any request they may have as we listen to the Holy Spirit. Part of listening is asking any questions to help clarify and fully understand the specifics of their request, as much as they are willing to share.

Treat each prayer request with honor and give gentle respect to the one asking for prayer.

A gentle physical touch while we pray helps soften the heart, inviting their heart to be one that is willing to receive from God. So, we ask permission to place a hand on them, typically on their shoulder. If physical healing is needed, we ask to place our hand on the wound, if it is appropriate. We listen and pray blessing, healing, deliverance, prophecy or anything else that the Holy Spirit leads us to pray.

John 13:35 NLT Your love for one another will prove to the world that you are my disciples.

We pray boldly, with the authority of heaven, by the power of the name of Jesus Christ. We pray confidently, being led by the Holy Spirit and standing on the Word of God. We pray without compromise, full of the completeness of the love of God. We express the love Christ has for them as we pray and encourage them in our prayers. We speak any prophetic words of encouragement the Holy Spirit has given us for them.

It is our love for others that sets us apart. It is the love of Jesus Christ living in us that gives us the eyes to see others the way He sees them.

In prayer we activate the gifts and power of heaven to move in the lives of those we love. We pray for salvation of our friends and family members that are lost. We pray for God to move in our community in miraculous ways. We pray for healing for those we know are sick and dying. We pray for deliverance for those that are oppressed and lost in the trap of the enemy. We pray for freedom for those around us, proclaiming victory over the enemy who is trying to destroy us. We pray to be used by God to reach more people for His Kingdom.

When Jesus would look over the crowds of people, He had compassion over them. In Matthew 9 we read that Jesus saw the people as being confused and helpless, "like sheep without a shepherd." (v 36 NLT)

Matthew 9:37-38 NLT – He said to His disciples, "the harvest is great, but the workers are few. So pray to the Lord of the harvest; ask Him to send more workers into His fields"

We need more workers in the fields. We need more prayers to establish God's Word into the hearts of the lost. We need more prayer warriors to battle against the schemes of the enemy. We need more prayer champions to proclaim the victory of the Good News, given by God in His Word and the encouraging words from the Holy Spirit. We need those that will stand together, fully alert, praying for others and each other. Praying at all times, on every occasion, releasing the Holy Spirit into our homes and our community.

Get in the Field!

Name those that are lost and are desperately in need of connection with God.

_____

_____

Ask God to reveal the greatest need in their lives, the thing that is holding them from turning to Jesus:

_____

_____

Write a prayer to heal, break through or repent for them and encourage them in that prayer:

Write and share with others how they can be praying for you. Be specific and trust your fellow prayer champions:

_____

_____

Prayer Habits.

It takes 21 days of consistent work to build a habit. Here are some vital prayer habits to build on. I encourage you, I challenge you, to establish these habits in your daily life and see what God does in your life.

Listening Prayer

Spend 15 minutes resting in silence and listening to God's voice.

S — M — T — W — T — F — S
S — M — T — W — T — F — S
S — M — T — W — T — F — S

Pray God's Word

Write a verse of the day into a prayer of the day.

S — M — T — W — T — F — S
S — M — T — W — T — F — S
S — M — T — W — T — F — S

Prayer for the Lost

List and pray for those who are lost and need the Holy Spirit to lead them to Jesus.

S — M — T — W — T — F — S
S — M — T — W — T — F — S
S — M — T — W — T — F — S

Pray Repentance

Ask the Holy Spirit to reveal veils between you and God. Repent and surrender them to Jesus.

S — M — T — W — T — F — S
S — M — T — W — T — F — S
S — M — T — W — T — F — S

Pray Forgiveness

Ask God to reveal any unforgiveness you have, and lay it down.

S — M — T — W — T — F — S
S — M — T — W — T — F — S
S — M — T — W — T — F — S

Truth Library.

Find Bible verses that state who you are in Christ, and proclaim that truth over yourself. Have this list ready for when the enemy tries to call you something that you are not.

Verse
_____
_____
_____
_____

I am:

Verse
_____
_____
_____
_____

I am:

Verse
_____
_____
_____
_____

I am:

Verse
_____
_____
_____
_____

I am:

Daily Prayer.

Truths:

_____

_____

_____

_____

_____

_____

_____

_____

_____

_____

Verse:

Prophetic Word:

Name, Word & Verse

_____

_____

_____

Name, Word & Verse

_____

_____

_____

_____

_____

_____

Weekly Prayers.

Write the theme or focus of your daily prayers for each week. Review what you have heard throughout the month and where you have seen victory.

Week 01 _____

_____

Week 02 _____

_____

Week 03 _____

_____

Week 04 _____

_____

Victories

_____

_____

_____

_____

Verse of the Month:

Recomendations &
Endorsements

Pastor Marty Schmidt
Lead Pastor
The Bridge Church, Ottumwa, Iowa

"The concept of prayer is not lost on many and yet it is a deep and vast mystery. What prayer is, conversing with God, makes sense. What to pray and how to pray is a different story. It is in the journey of what to pray that we learn that prayer is as comforting as a child holding a teddy bear and as wild as wrestling with a grizzly bear in nature. What Ben Foote has put together in, Pray What!?, is a marvelous gift. For the one who is looking for a 101 on where to start with prayer, here is your guide, to the one who is looking to go deeper and further in prayer, the one looking for a 401 class, here is your guide. That is why this book is so amazing. It is accessible and profound. I'm so excited for you the reader to not just read, but mark up, ponder, and most of all practice the various aspects of prayer laid out in the chapters ahead."

Pastor Jacob Wilson
Campus Pastor
The Bridge Church, Ottumwa, Iowa

"Ben Foote's 'Prayer What!?' is a refreshing and insightful journey into the heart of prayer. It's practical, thought provoking, and Scripture focused. Whether you're a seasoned prayer warrior or just beginning to explore the power of prayer, this book will inspire and equip you to deepen your connection with God and experience the transformative power of prayer in your daily life. A must-read for anyone longing for an authentic prayer life and to cultivate a richer, more meaningful relationship with our speaking God."

Trevor Bunch, PhD
Adjunct Instructor of Computing and Information Science
Messiah University

"Ben's practical steps through how to pray in a way that both encourage and challenge us to approach praying with thankfulness, humility, and boldness. This book is a very accessible resource for launching or maturing a prayer ministry; however, don't underestimate its ability to round out aspects of your personal prayer life during the process."

Aprile Goodman
Prayer Team - Home Blessing Coordinator
The Bridge Church, Ottumwa, Iowa

James 5:16, "The prayer of a righteous man is powerful and effective." Pray What!? is a Holy Spirit led book written by Ben Foote. Pray What!? guides us in our prayer journey with God whether you are new to prayer or an experienced prayer warrior, you will return to this book again and again for guidance in blessing thow you pray for and for your own relationship with God.

References

Holy Bible, New Living Translation, copyright 1996, 2004, 2015 by Tynsdal House foundation.

The ESV Bible (The Holy Bible, English Standard Version) copyright 2001 by Crossway Bibles, a publishing ministry of Good News Publishers.

Training Modules, Wellsprings of Freedom International AFP, by Rev. Tim Howard and Rev. Brian Burks, 2nd edition, 2018

Equipped for Battle, Samuel M Kaswalya, Bethel Community Outreach Ministries, Uganada, UK

Pray

What!?

WORD   VOICE   REPENT   FORGIVE   WARFARE   HEAL   PROPHECY   SPIRIT   LEAD

Written by Ben Foote
From Armor Up Prayer
Produced by Tony and Laura Broullire, and Ten Talents Design Studio

WestBow Press books may be ordered through booksellers or by contacting:

WestBow Press
A Division of Thomas Nelson & Zondervan
1663 Liberty Drive
Bloomington, IN 47403
www.westbowpress.com
844-714-3454

NLT – New Living Translation
Scripture quotations taken from the Holy Bible, New Living Translation, Copyright © 1996, 2004. Used
by permission of Tyndale House Publishers, Inc., Wheaton, Illinois 60189. All rights reserved.

ESV – English Standard Version
Scripture quotations are from The Holy Bible, English Standard Version® (ESV®), copyright © 2001 by
Crossway, a publishing ministry of Good News Publishers. Used by permission. All rights reserved.

ISBN: 979-8-3850-3315-7 (sc)
ISBN: 979-8-3850-3316-4 (hc)
ISBN: 979-8-3850-3317-1 (e)

Library of Congress Control Number: 2024918663

Print information available on the last page.

WestBow Press rev. date: 09/13/2024

WESTBOW
PRESS®
A DIVISION OF THOMAS NELSON
& ZONDERVAN

Printed in the United States
by Baker & Taylor Publisher Services